BERNARD C. NALTY

RIGHT to FIGHT

AFRICAN-AMERICAN MARINES IN WWII

Published by Orison Publishers, Inc in partnership with Utley Associates
www.BlacksinWWii.com

The Right to Fight: African-American Marines in World War II

by Bernard C. Nalty

young white Marine, Edward Andrusko of Company I, 7th Marines, saw his first black Leathernecks as he crossed the beach at Peleliu in September 1944, returning to the fight after having his wounds treated at a hospital ship offshore. The African-Americans were transferring ammunition from landing craft onto trucks and delivering it to the front lines. Handling ammunition struck him as "a dangerous task at any time," but with enemy shells churning the coral sands, "it was a heroic, thankless job that few of us wanted." The black driver of one of the trucks offered a ride inland, and Andrusko accepted, taking his place in the cab, with a cargo of high explosives behind him. As the sound of battle drew nearer, he concluded that he had made "a stupid and dangerous choice of transportation," but he reached his unit safely.

Andrusko again saw the African-American Marines after his company, advancing through the island's rugged terrain, encountered concealed Japanese positions and came under fire that pinned the men down. With the company's first sergeant and another Marine, he set out to find riflemen to take the place of casualties and stretcher bearers to carry off the wounded and dead. The first Marines that Andrusko and the others found proved to be members of the

---

On the Cover: *A veteran 90mm crew of the 51st Defense Battalion poses with its gun, "Lena Horne," at Eniwetok in 1945.* Department of Defense Photo (USMC) 121743

At left: *Men of Montford Point clear an obstacle on the way to earning the right to serve in the U.S. Marine Corps.*

---

very unit he had met on the beach, and the blacks immediately volunteered to help. Andrusko's first sergeant had no idea that African-Americans were serving in the Marine Corps, so complete was the segregation of the races, but he welcomed their aid. The black Marines moved forward to the tangled ridges where Company I was fighting, carried away the casualties during the afternoon—one of the wounded compared them to "black angels sent by God"—and manned empty foxholes to help beat back a nighttime Japanese counterattack.

When Andrusko encountered the men of the ammunition company, few white Marines knew that African-Americans had been serving in the Corps for more than two years. The leadership of the Marine Corps had shown scant enthusiasm for accepting African-Americans, who had to overcome the barrier of racial prejudice as they struggled for the right to serve. But serve they did, ably and gallantly.

Basic Racial Policy

When the United States began arming against aggression by the Axis powers—Nazi Germany, Imperial Japan, and Fascist Italy—the Marine Corps had a simple and inflexible policy governing African-Americans: it had not accepted them since its reestablishment in 1798 and did not want them now. In April 1941, during a meeting of the General Board of the Navy—a body roughly comparable to the War Department General Staff—the Commandant of the Marine Corps, Major General Thomas Holcomb, declared that blacks had no place in the organization he headed. "If it were a question of having a Marine Corps

of 5,000 whites or 250,000 Negroes," he said, "I would rather have the whites."

Whereas General Holcomb and the Marine Corps refused to accept African-Americans, the Navy admitted blacks in small numbers, but only to serve as messmen or stewards. The forces of change were gathering momentum, however. President Franklin D. Roosevelt, after meeting in September 1940 with a panel of black leaders, offered African-Americans better treatment and greater opportunity within the segregated armed forces in return for their support of his rearmament program and his attempt to gain an unprecedented third term in the November Presidential election. Roosevelt won that election with the help of those blacks, mainly in the cities of the North, who could still exercise the right to vote, and he did so without antagonizing the Southern segregationists in the Senate and House of Representatives whose support he needed for his anti-Nazi foreign policy.

By the spring of 1941, many black leaders felt that the time had come for the Roosevelt administration to make good its pledge to African-Americans, repaying them for their help. A. Philip Randolph, president of the Brotherhood of Sleeping Car Porters, a union made up exclusively of blacks, forcefully reminded the Chief Executive of this promise, threatening a march on Washington by as many as 100,000 African-Americans who would demand their rights as citizens. Roosevelt forestalled the march by issuing in June an executive order banning racial discrimination in hiring by defense industries under contract to the federal

African-Americans and the Marines

The estimated 5,000 blacks, free men and slaves, who served the American cause in the Revolutionary War included at least a few Continental Marines. For example, in April 1776 Captain Miles Pennington, Marine officer of the Continental brig *Reprisal*, recruited a slave, John Martin (also known as Keto), without obtaining permission from the slaveholder, William Marshall of Wilmington, Delaware. Private Martin participated in a cruise that resulted in the capture of five British merchantmen, but died in October 1777, along with all but one of his shipmates, when *Reprisal* foundered in a gale.

Two other blacks, Isaac Walker and a man known only as Orange, enlisted at Philadelphia's Tun Tavern in a company raised by Robert Mullan, the owner of the tavern, which served as a recruiting rendezvous for Marines. Captain Mullan's company, part of a battalion raised by Major Samuel Nicholas, crossed the Delaware River with George Washington on Christmas Eve 1776 and fought the British at Princeton. The wartime contributions of the black Continental Marines, and the other blacks who served on land or at sea, went unrewarded, for the armed forces of the independent United States sought to exclude African-Americans.

For a time, a militia backed by a small regular Army—both made up exclusively of whites—seemed force enough to defend the nation, but tensions between the United States and France resulted in the building of a fleet to replace the disbanded Continental Navy. In 1798, when the time arrived to recruit crews for the new warships, the Navy banned "Negroes or Mulattoes," grouping them with "Persons whose Characters are Suspicious." The Commandant of the reestablished Marine Corps, Lieutenant Colonel William Ward Burrows, followed the Navy's example and barred African-Americans from enlisting, although black drummers and fifers might provide music to attract potential recruits.

The Marine Corps maintained this racial exclusiveness until World War II. Its small size enabled the Corps to recruit enough whites to fill its ranks, but other considerations may also have helped shape racial policy. Marines maintained order on shipboard and at naval installations, and the idea of blacks exercising authority over white sailors would have shocked a racially conscious America. The Marine Corps, moreover, had a sizable proportion of Southern officers, products of a society that had held black slaves. Not even the Northern victory in the Civil War, which enforced emancipation, could bring the races together in the former Confederacy. Jim Crow, the personification of racial segregation, rapidly imposed his grip on the entire nation, assuming the force of law in 1896 when the Supreme Court decided *Plessy v. Ferguson* and, in effect, isolated blacks from white society.

government and establishing the Fair Employment Practices Commission to monitor compliance. He also increased pressure on the armed forces to provide blacks better treatment and broader opportunities as he had pledged during the previous autumn.

The naval establishment had been slow to carry out the President's wishes. As late as the summer of 1941, Secretary of the Navy Frank Knox continued to oppose the recruiting of African-Americans, except as stewards in officers' messes. He insisted that the restrictions on opportunities actually benefited blacks, for in other specialties they would have to compete on equal terms with whites and could not possibly succeed. Since the President, an Assistant Secretary of the Navy during World War I, took a personal interest in the Navy and Marine Corps, Knox realized these services would have to lower their racial barriers and reluctantly suggested recruiting 5,000 blacks for general service. In January 1942, while the General Board considered this proposal and reflected on the presidential pressure behind it, General Holcomb voiced his deeply felt misgivings. Although further opposition could only be futile, the Commandant complained that those blacks seeking to enlist in the Marine Corps were "trying to break into a club that doesn't want them." The "negro race," he argued, "has every opportunity now to satisfy its aspirations for combat in the Army," which had maintained four regular regiments of black soldiers since shortly after the Civil War.

Roosevelt tried to avoid antagonizing a reluctant Navy, offering assurance that it need not "go all the way at one fell swoop" and racially integrate the general service. He kept pushing, however, for greater opportunities for blacks within the bounds of segregation, and the Navy could not defy the Commander in Chief. Secretary Knox on 7 April 1942 advised the uniformed leaders of the Navy, Marine Corps, and Coast Guard (a component of the wartime Navy) that they would have to accept African-Americans for general service. Some six weeks later, the Navy Department publicly announced that the Navy, Marine Corps, and Coast Guard would enlist about 1,000 African-Americans each month, beginning 1 June, and that the Marines would organize a racially segregated 900-man defense battalion, training the blacks recruited for it from the beginning of boot camp onward.

Change Comes to the Marine Corps

On 25 May 1942 the Commandant of the Marine Corps issued formal instructions to begin on 1 June to

Painting by Col Charles H. Waterhouse, USMCR (Ret.)

A black American served with the Marines when Gen George Washington fought the Battle of Princeton in January 1777.

recruit qualified "colored male citizens of the United States between the ages of 17 and 29, inclusive, for service in a combat organization." Given the nature of American society in 1942, that organization would be racially segregated, the blacks in the ranks being commanded by whites. Those black volunteers whom the Marine Corps accepted would, as most wartime white recruits, enter the reserve for the duration of the war plus six months, but their active duty would be delayed until the completion of a segregated training camp, scheduled for 25 July. Some of the new recruits would serve as specialists, everything from cooks to clerks, who would see to the day-to-day operation of a racially exclusive training camp.

The task of forming and training even one battalion of African-Americans seemed a formidable challenge, for it involved giving raw recruits their basic skills, further honing the fighting edge, and finally creating a combat team. General Ray A. Robinson, in 1942 a colonel in charge of the Personnel Section, Division of Plans and Policies, at Marine Corps headquarters, confessed during an interview in 1968 that the admission of blacks "just scared us to death." Although the draft did not become the normal source of recruits for all the services until December 1942, and the first draftees did not enter the Marine Corps until January 1943, Robinson sought help from the Selective Service System, where a black officer of the Army Reserve, Lieutenant Colonel Campbell C. Johnson, had been called to active duty as an administrator. Johnson indicated that he would do what he could and joked about passing the word that Marines die young, so that only those African-Americans willing to risk their lives would join. Robinson acknowledged that the Corps "got some awfully good Negroes" over the years and believed that Johnson was at least partly responsible.

Despite Johnson's interest in the black Marines, the Corps had to rely throughout 1942 on volunteers, and recruiting proved sluggish. By mid-June, only 63 African-Americans had enlisted and recruiters were becoming desperate, since the training camp for blacks neared completion. This lack of immediate results reflected the fact that the Marine Corps, after excluding African-Americans since the American Revolution, was attempting to sign up recruits in a black community that had no tradition of service as Leathernecks. Recruiters found it especially difficult to sign up the truck drivers, cooks, and typists to support the battalion, even though black educators assured the Marine Corps that an adequate pool of such specialists existed. When a recruiter in Boston told Obie Hall that he could enter the Marine Corps immediately if he had the right specialty, Hall said he was a truck driver. Although he "no more could drive a truck than the man in the moon," he wanted to go and had no hope of passing himself off as a cook or typist.

The number of African-Americans who shared Hall's enthusiasm slowly increased. Some of those who joined up looked on serving in the Marine Corps as an opportunity denied blacks for a century and a half. Others saw this service as a personal challenge. By the end of September, about half of the 1,200 recruits needed to man the battalion and render administrative, housekeeping, and transportation support had enlisted. The Presidential decision on 1 December 1942 to make the Selective Service System the normal source of recruits for all the services ensured that, beginning in January 1943, 1,000 African-Americans would enter the Marine Corps each month. This influx resulted from the fact that the draft law prohibited racial discrimination in its administration; in practical terms, this meant that the Army and Navy could establish quotas for black recruits but not arbitrarily exclude them.

While preparing to absorb the African-Americans provided by the Selective Service System, the Marine Corps reaffirmed its commitment to racial segregation, but it proposed to carry out this policy without channeling blacks into meaningless assignments that had little to do with winning the war. Lacking recent experience with blacks, the Marines sought to profit from the example of the Army, which avoided placing blacks in charge of whites. Applying this lesson, General Holcomb in March 1943 issued Letter of Instruction 421, which declared it "essential that in no case shall there be colored noncommissioned officers senior to white men in the same unit, and desirable that few, if any, be of the same rank." LOI 421 was a classified document and did not become public during the war, but the African-American Marine who could not earn promotion because a white noncommissioned officer blocked his path immediately felt its impact. To remove this racial roadblock while adhering to the policy of segregation, white noncommissioned officers would be removed as promptly and completely as feasible from the newly organized black units, forcing the Marine Corps to create in a matter of months a fully functioning cadre of black sergeants and corporals.

At best, the Commandant had mixed feelings about the black recruits whom the Roosevelt administration had forced on him. "All Marines," he proclaimed, "are entitled to the same rights and privileges under Navy Regulations," but even as he announced this idealistic principle, he felt compelled to remind the African-Americans that they should "conduct themselves with propriety and become a real credit to the Corps" and to require periodic reports on their status. The black Marines clearly faced a struggle for acceptance within the Corps before they got the opportunity to fight the Japanese.

Cpl Edgar R. Huff drills a platoon of recruits at the Montford Point Camp. He enlisted in the Marine Corps in June 1942. *Huff became a legend among the Marines who were trained here. He retired in 1972 as a sergeant major at New River.*

National Archives Photo 127-N-5337

Service in the Marine Corps brought men like Obie Hall, who enlisted from the cities of the North where race relations were somewhat relaxed, into contact with segregation at its harshest. Hall received a sleeping-car ticket for the rail journey from Boston to the training site in North Carolina, and all went well until he reached Washington, D.C., where he was ordered out of his assigned berth. A porter, also an African-American, explained that Hall had reached the "black line" south of which rail travel was segregated. The porter, in defiance of the law and social custom of that time, found an empty compartment that Hall occupied for the rest of the trip. Some 18 months later, John R. Griffin of Chicago did not find a sympathetic porter willing to break the rules; at Washington he had to transfer to a Jim Crow car, "hot, dirty, crowded (with babies crying and old men drinking and [black] Marines discussing the fun they had on leave)."

Segregation prevailed at the Marine Barracks, New River, North Carolina — soon redesignated Camp Lejeune — where the African-Americans would train, and in the nearby town of Jacksonville. For the black recruits, the Marine Corps established a separate cantonment, the Montford Point Camp, in western-most Camp Lejeune. At least one Marine veteran, Lieutenant General James L. Underhill, suggested in retrospect that the Corps made a mistake in pushing them "off to one corner," for doing so reinforced the belief, accurate though it was, that blacks were not truly welcome. The Marine Corps, Underhill believed, "should have dressed them up in blue uniforms and put them behind a band and marched them down Fifth Avenue" to show their pride in being Marines and their acceptance by the Corps. At the time, as Underhill surely realized, neither the Marine Corps

Department of Defense Photo (USMC) 5344

Sgt Gilbert H. "Hashmark" Johnson, a veteran of service in both the Army and Navy, glares at the boots in his recruit platoon. He became a Marine in 1942.

nor much of American society was ready for such a gesture of racial amity.

The Montford Point Camp consisted at first of a headquarters building, a chapel, two warehouses, a mess hall, a dispensary, a steam generating plant, a motor pool, quarters and recreational facilities for the white enlisted men who initially staffed the operation, a barber shop, and 120 green-painted prefabricated huts, each capable of accommodating 16 recruits, though twice that number were sometimes jammed into them, pending the completion of new barracks. The original camp also boasted a snack bar that dispensed beer, a small club for the white officers, and a theater, one wing of which was converted into a library. As the black Marines cleared the land around the camp, they encountered clouds of mosquitoes, a variety of snakes, and the tracks of an occasional bear, if not the animal itself. To the north of the original site, across a creek, lay Camp Knox, occupied during the Great Depression of the 1930s by a contingent of the Civilian Conservation Corps, an agency that put jobless young men to work, under military supervision, on public improvements and recla-

mation projects. As the number of African-American Marines increased, they spilled over into the old CCC camp.

Railroad tracks divided white residents from black in segregated Jacksonville. Suddenly, hundreds of African-American Marines on liberty appeared on the white side of the tracks, looking for entertainment. At first, white businessmen reacted to this sight by bolting their doors. Even the bus depot shut down until someone realized that the liberty parties might well find other North Carolina towns like New Bern or Wilmington more attractive than Jacksonville, and the ticket agents went back to work.

Getting out of Jacksonville became easier, but returning to camp from the town proved difficult on a Jim Crow bus line. Drivers gave priority to white passengers, as state law required, and restricted black passengers to the rear of the bus, unless whites needed the space. Since the two races formed separate lines at the bus stop, drivers tended to take only whites on board and leave the black Marines standing there as the deadline for returning to Montford Point drew nearer. When this happened, angry black Marines, at the risk of

The 'Great White Father'

Colonel Samuel A. Woods, Jr., launched the training program for black Marines at Montford (originally Mumford) Point. At this time, based on the Army's practices, the Marine Corps believed that officers born in the South were uniquely suited to commanding African-Americans, and the colonel fit the pattern, since he hailed from South Carolina. Born at Arlington, he graduated from The Citadel, South Carolina's military college, and in 1906 accepted a commission in the Corps. He served in Haiti and Cuba but arrived in France as World War I was ending. Afterward he saw duty in the Dominican Republic and China, attended the Naval War College, and headed the Marine Corps correspondence schools at the Marine Barracks, Quantico, Virginia.

The colonel's calmness and fairness earned him the respect of the blacks he commanded. He cultivated a paternalistic relationship with his men and emerged, according to one African-American veteran of the Montford Point Camp, as "the Great White Father of everybody," trying to ease the impact of segregation on the morale of his troops, though he accepted the separation of the races, and insisting that the black Marines exhibit self-pride and competence.

National Archives Photo 127-N-9511
Col Samuel A. Woods, Jr., established the Montford Point Camp and also served as the first commanding officer of the 51st Defense Battalion (Composite).

violence from the local police, might commandeer a bus, remove the driver, and take it to the gate nearest Jacksonville, where the transit company could retrieve it on the next morning. The white officer in command at Montford Point, Colonel Samuel A. Woods, Jr., took steps to ensure that the black Marines could return safely to Montford Point without risking arrest. He sent his battalion's trucks into town to pick up the men and assigned white noncommissioned officers from the staff at Montford Point to the military police patrols that kept order in the town. The NCOs detailed by Colonel Woods helped deter local authorities from making arbitrary arrests of black Marines. As black noncommissioned officers became available, one of them accompanied each patrol, though unarmed and without authority to arrest or detain white Marines.

Although race also affected relationships among Marines, especially during the early months of the Montford Point Camp, instances of the racial harassment of black Marines became increasingly less frequent. The improved conditions resulted in part from Montford Point's isolation, but it also reflected the efforts of the African-Americans to impress their white fellow Marines. Obie Hall recalled that the men of Montford Point tried to look their sharpest, especially when in the presence of white Marines. "They really put that chest out," he said. Pride in appearance had beneficial effects, for one white Marine remarked that, although he only saw blacks when they were on liberty because of the segregation on Camp Lejeune, "they always looked sharp." The white military police remained unimpressed, however. They tended to share the racial attitudes of their civilian counterparts, and the persistent hostility generated intense resentment among the African-American Marines.

Knowledge that they would have to overcome racism to gain the right to serve created a feeling of solidarity among black Marines. At times, they could invoke this unity to right a wrong, as happened after the officer of the day at Montford Point, angered by what he considered raucous behavior during a comedy being shown at the camp movie theater, had the black audience take their buckets—these utilitarian possessions at the time were serving as seats—and put them over their heads. The recently appointed black drill instructors reacted by ordering their Marines to clean the barracks instead of attending a show being staged especially for them by black performers. When Colonel Woods heard of the impromptu field day, he investigated, learned of the ill-considered action by the officer of the day, and made sure the African-Americans attended the performance.

One incident painfully reminded the African-Americans of their second-class status in the Marine Corps, indeed throughout a Jim Crow society. A boxing show staged at the Montford Point Camp attracted a distinguished guest, Major General Henry L. Larsen, who had taken command of Camp Lejeune after returning from the South Pacific. During an informal talk, he made what he considered a humorous remark, but his audience interpreted it as an insult. According to one of the black Marines who was there, the general said something to the effect that when he returned from overseas he had seen women Marines and dog Marines, but when he saw "you people wearing our uniform," he knew there was a war on. The off-hand comment may have served, however, to bring the men of Montford Point even closer together.

Oddly enough, a white officer came the closest to capturing the isolation felt by blacks in segregated North Carolina. Robert W. Troup, in peacetime a musician and composer who had played alongside black performers, accepted a wartime commission and reported to Montford Point, where he made a lasting impression. One of the African-American Marines, Gilbert H. Johnson, considered him a "topnotch musician, a very decent sort of officer," and another, Obie Hall, described him as "the sharpest cat I've ever seen in my life." Bobby Troup's song "Jacksonville," the unofficial anthem of men of Montford Point, included the heartfelt plea:

> Take me away from Jacksonville, 'cause I've had my fill and that's no lie.
>
> Take me away from Jacksonville, keep me away from Jacksonville until I die. Jacksonville stood still, while the rest of the world passed by.

While assigned to the 51st Defense Battalion (Composite), the African-American defense battalion authorized in 1942, Troup doubled as recreation officer, organizing baseball and basketball teams, arranging the construction of sports facilities, and staging shows using talent available at Montford Point. Perhaps the most popular performer was Finis Henderson, a private who had sung and tapdanced in Metro-Goldwyn-Mayer films. As the star of one of Troup's shows, Henderson sang "Jacksonville" while stage hands threw bits of brown paper into the air flow from a pair of electric fans to simulate the dust blowing down the street of that much-despised town. In December 1944, Troup took command of the black 6th Depot Company—the second unit with that designation—which deployed to Saipan and handled supplies at the base there.

Starting from Scratch

The training program at Montford Point, which signaled the first appearance of blacks in Marine uniforms since the Revolutionary War, began with boot camp and had as its ultimate objective the creation of a composite defense battalion. This combat unit would be racially segregated, commanded by white officers, and with an initial complement of white noncommissioned officers, who would serve only until black replacements became available. Colonel Woods had to start from scratch, with no cadre of experienced African-Americans except for a handful with prior service in the Army or Navy. When boot training began, the colonel commanded both the camp itself and the 51st Defense Battalion (Composite) being formed there. Lieutenant Colonel Theodore A. Holdahl—an enlisted veteran of World War I who served as an officer in the Far East and Central America—had charge of recruit training. Some two dozen white officers, a number of them recently commissioned second lieutenants like Bobby Troup, and 90 white enlisted Marines, directed the training. The enlisted men formed the Special Enlisted Staff, which initially carried out assignments that varied from clerk or typist to drill instructor. The Marine Corps screened the Special Enlisted Staff to exclude anyone opposed to the presence of blacks in the ranks. One of the Montford Point Marines suggested that, in the normal pressures of boot camp, a breakdown in the screening process could have doomed the program, for racial hostility would have reinforced the usual harassment visited on every recruit, white or black. "We would all have left the first week," he joked. "Some of us, probably, the first night."

In keeping with Marine Corps policy, Woods and Holdahl had to replace the whites of the Special Enlisted Staff with black noncommissioned officers as rapidly as possible. The command structure at Montford Point tried to identify the best of the African-American recruits and place

Bobby Troup, a musician turned wartime Marine Corps officer, staged shows at Montford Point using talent such as Private Finis Henderson, a professional singer and dancer before enlisting, and Curtis Institute graduate Sgt Joe Wilder, not shown.
Department of Defense Photo (USMC) 6797

These Marines of the first platoon to enter recruit training at Montford Point were promoted to private first class a month before they completed boot camp and became assistant drill instructors. From left are Mortimer A. Cox; Arnold R. Bostick; Edgar R. Davis, Jr.; Gilbert H. "Hashmark" Johnson and Edgar R. Huff (their drill instructors); and Charles E. Allen.

them on a fast track to positions of responsibility in boot camp and in the battalion itself. The general classification test, administered as a part of the initial processing, grouped those who took the test into five categories, with the highest scores in Category I, and afforded one tool for predicting the ability of the new Marines. Unfortunately, those black Marines who administered the test and interpreted the results were themselves on-the-job trainees. Consequently, the test results could at times prove misleading, with college graduates sometimes showing up in Categories IV or even V. Drill instructors, initially whites with varying experience in the Marine Corps, had to rely on their own powers of observation to determine which of the African-American recruits had the aptitude to exercise effective leadership and master the necessary technology. Formal tests, written or

oral, provided a final winnowing of the candidates. The first promotions, to private first class, took place early in November 1942, a month before the men selected to sew on their single stripe had completed boot camp.

The problem of classifying recruits demonstrated that the Montford Point Camp required skilled administrators. Creating an administrative infrastructure proved difficult, for the comparatively few volunteers who stepped forward in the summer and fall of 1942 included few clerks and typists. Enough African-American recruits would have to learn the mysteries of Marine Corps administration to fill the necessary billets, but racial segregation prevented them from taking courses alongside whites. For the present, white instructors would teach administrative subjects at Montford Point, until black Marines could master the skills and pass

them along. When tackling the more complex subjects, like optical fire control or radar, the African-Americans attended courses offered by the Army at nearby Camp Davis, North Carolina, and elsewhere.

Lacking a cadre of black veterans, the Marine Corps had to advance the best of the African-American recruits into the ranks of noncommissioned officers so as to achieve the goal of a segregated defense battalion commanded by white officers but with no white enlisted men in any capacity. The promotion of black Marines depended on ability, as revealed by the initial classification tests, ratings from superiors, the results of formal examinations, and the existence of vacancies that would not violate policy by placing a black Marine in charge of whites. As the number of African-American Marines increased and training activity accelerated, some of the recently promoted pri-

Two of Those Who Succeeded

Two of the black Marines who overcame every challenge, Edgar R. Huff and Gilbert H. Johnson, became legends among the men of Montford Point. Both grew up in Alabama, and ultimately would marry twin sisters, but their military backgrounds could not have been more different. Huff's service began when he joined the Marine Corps, but Johnson had served in both the Army and Navy before he reported to Montford Point.

Gilbert H. Johnson earned the nickname "Hashmark" because he wore on the sleeve of his Marine Corps uniform three of the diagonal stripes, called hashmarks, indicating successful previous enlistments. Born in Mt. Hebron, Alabama, in 1905, he joined the Army in 1923 and served two three-year hitches with a black regiment, the 25th Infantry. In 1933, he enlisted in the Naval Reserve as a mess attendant, serving on active duty in officers' messes at various installations in Texas. He entered the regular Navy in May 1941 and had become a steward second class by 1942 when he heard that the Marine Corps was recruiting African-Americans.

With infantry experience ranging from company clerk to mortar gunner and squad leader, Johnson felt he was ideally suited to become a Marine. As regulations required, he applied to the Secretary of the Navy, via the Commandant of the Marine Corps, for a discharge from the Navy in order to join the Marines. He received the necessary permission and reported to Montford Point on 14 November 1942, still wearing his steward's uniform.

As he anticipated, he possessed vitally needed skills that resulted in his being chosen as an assistant drill instructor and later a drill instructor. He ended up supervising the very platoon in which he had started his training. Looking back on his days as a DI, Johnson conceded that he was something of an "ogre" on the drill field. "I was a stern instructor," he said, "but I was fair." He sought, with unswerving dedication, to produce "in a few weeks, and at most a few months, a type of Marine fully qualified in every respect to wear that much cherished Globe and Anchor." In January 1945, he became sergeant major of the Montford Point Camp and in June of that year joined the 52d Defense Battalion on Guam, also as sergeant major, remain-

ing in that assignment until the unit disbanded in 1946.

His subsequent career included service during the Korean War. He retired in 1955 after completing a tour of duty as First Sergeant, Headquarters and Service Company, 3d Marines, 3d Marine Division. He died in 1972. Two years afterward, the Marine Corps paid tribute to his accomplishments by redesignating the Montford Point Camp as Camp Gilbert H. Johnson.

Edgar R. Huff enlisted in the Marine Corps in June 1942 and underwent training at the new Montford Point Camp. "I wanted to be a Marine," he said years later, "because I had always heard that the Marine Corps was the toughest outfit going, and I felt I was the toughest going, so I wanted to be a member of the best organization." His toughness and physical strength had served him well while a crane rigger for the Republic Steel Company in Alabama City, near his home town of Gadsden, Alabama.

Huff reported for duty at a time when the Montford Point operation desperately needed forceful and intelligent African-Americans, with or without previous military experience, to take over from the white noncommissioned officers of the Special Enlisted Staff. Since he possessed the very qualities that the Marine Corps was seeking, he attended a drill instructor's course, served briefly as an assistant to two white drill instructors, took over a platoon of his own, and soon assumed responsibility for all the DIs at Montford Point He made platoon sergeant in September 1943, gunnery sergeant in November of that year, and in June 1944 became first sergeant of a malaria control detachment at Montford Point. He went overseas six months later as the first sergeant of the 5th Depot Company — the second wartime unit with that designation — served on Saipan, saw combat on Okinawa, and took part in the occupation of North China.

Discharged from the Marine Corps when the war ended, he spent a few months as a civilian and then reenlisted. He saw service in the Korean War and the Vietnam War. During his second tour of duty in Vietnam, he was Sergeant Major, III Marine Amphibious Force, the principal Marine Corps command in Southeast Asia. He retired in 1972 while Sergeant Major, Marine Corps Air Station, New River, North Carolina, and died in May 1994.

Gilbert H. "Hashmark" Johnson
Department of Defense Photo (USMC) 5344

Edgar R. Huff

National Archives Photo 127-N-5334

During a demonstration while training at Montford Point, Cpl Arvin L. "Tony" Ghazlo, instructor in unarmed combat, disarms his assistant, PFC Ernest Jones.

vates first class, corporals, and sergeants became assistant drill instructors at the Montford Point boot camp, replaced the white drill instructors, or joined the defense battalion when it began taking shape. The rapid expansion of the noncommissioned ranks thrust many of the newly promoted black Marines into sink-or-swim assignments in which they not only kept their heads above water but made rapid progress against the current.

A few of the black volunteers besides Gilbert Johnson had previous military experience; others had special ability or the potential for leadership. John T. Pridgen, for instance, had served in the 10th Cavalry before the war, and George A. Jackson had been an officer in the peacetime Army reserve. At a time when few whites and fewer blacks held degrees, the Montford Point Marines included several college graduates, among them Charles F. Anderson and Charles W. Simmons. The talents of Arvin L. "Tony" Ghazlo proved as valuable as they were rare, for as a civilian he had given lessons in jujitsu. With the help of another black

Marine, Ernest "Judo" Jones, Ghazlo taught unarmed combat at Montford Point. Men like these replaced members of the Special Enlisted Staff in the training process, a transition all but completed by the end of April 1943, and became noncommissioned officers in the 51st Defense Battalion and the other units formed from the tide of draftees.

Thanks to the use of the Selective Service System as the normal source of recruits, the nature of the program at Montford Point was changing. A single defense battalion could not absorb the influx of blacks into the Marine Corps. Consequently, Secretary of the Navy Knox authorized a Marine Corps Messman Branch and the first of 63 combat support companies—either depot or ammunition units—as well as a second defense battalion, the 52d. An expansion of the Montford Point Camp began, as the Marine Corps prepared to house another thousand blacks there. The Headquarters and Service Company, Montford Point Camp, came into existence on 11 March 1943, and at the same time, the 51st Defense Battalion (Composite) provided the

nucleus for the Headquarters Company, Recruit Depot Battalion. Colonel Woods retained command of the camp, entrusting the defense battalion to Lieutenant Colonel W. Bayard Onley, a graduate of the Naval Academy whose most recent assignment had been Regimental Executive Officer, 23d Marines. Lieutenant Colonel Holdahl continued to exercise control over boot training as commander of the new recruit battalion. On 1 April, Captain Albert O. Madden, a veteran of World War I who, as a civilian, had operated restaurants in Albany, New York, took command of the new Messman Branch Battalion; on the 13th, when the Messman Branch became the Stewards' Branch, the name of Madden's battalion changed to reflect the redesignation. The growth of the Montford Point operation required additional housekeeping support, much of it obtained from the rifle company of the 51st Defense Battalion, after a modified table of organization disbanded the infantry unit in the summer of 1943.

Building the 51st Defense Battalion

The proliferation of African-American units and the expansion of activity at Montford Point interfered with the organization and training of the 51st Defense Battalion (Composite) by making demands on the pool of black noncommissioned officers that Woods, Holdahl, and the shrinking Special Enlisted Staff had assembled. The first, and for a time the only, Marine Corps combat unit to be manned by blacks found itself in competition with another defense battalion, the new combat support outfits (depot and ammunition companies), the Stewards' Branch, and, as before, the recruit training function. So thinly spread was the African-American enlisted leadership that the same individuals might serve in a succession of units. "Hashmark" Johnson, a DI in boot camp, ended

The Stewards' Branch

In organizing the Stewards' Branch, the Marine Corps followed the example of the Navy, which had begun before World War I to segregate the enlisted force by channeling blacks away from combat or technical specialties and making them stewards or mess attendants. Once Captain Madden's formal courses began producing enough graduates, the Stewards' Branch provided cooks and attendants for officers' messes in large-unit headquarters. Combat experience would prove that duty in the Stewards' Branch could be as dangerous as any other assignment open to blacks. On Saipan, for example, two members of the branch suffered wounds when the enemy shelled the headquarters of the 2d Marine Division. On Okinawa, where stewards routinely volunteered as stretcher bearers, Steward 2d Class Warren N. McGrew, Jr., was killed and seven others sustained wounds, one of them, Steward's Assistant 1st Class Joe N. Bryant, being wounded twice.

The Stewards' Branch did not include the cooks and bakers in black units. Segregation required that African-Americans take over these specialties, beginning at the Montford Point Camp. In January 1943, Jerome D. Alcorn, Otto Cherry, and Robert T. Davis became the first to cross the divide between assistant cook (at the time the equivalent of a corporal) and field cook (sergeant).

up with the 52d Defense Battalion. Similarly, Edgar Huff, also a DI, moved on to other assignments, including first sergeant of one of the combat service support companies.

The 51st had attained only half its authorized strength on 21 April, when a new commanding officer, Lieutenant Colonel Floyd A. Stephenson, took over from Lieutenant Colonel Onley. Stephenson, in command of a defense battalion at Pearl Harbor when the Japanese attacked, later declared that he "had no brief for the Negro program in the Marine Corps," since he hailed from Texas, "where matters relating to Negroes are normally given the closest critical scrutiny," a euphemistic description of Jim Crow. He was, in short, the product of a segregated society, but despite his background, he tackled his new assignment with enthusiasm and skill. African-Americans, he soon discovered, could learn to perform all the duties required in a defense battalion.

By the end of 1942, the nature of the defense battalion had begun changing. Already the Marine Corps had stricken light tanks from the table of organization and equipment, and, as close combat became increas-

ingly less likely, the rifle company and the pack howitzers followed the armor into oblivion. Emphasis shifted from repulsing amphibious landings to defending against Japanese air strikes and hit-and-run raids by warships. In June 1943, the qualifier "Composite" disappeared from the designation of the 51st Defense Battalion, the 155mm battery became a group, and the machine gun unit evolved into the Special Weapons Group, with 20mm and 40mm weapons, as well as machine guns. A month later, the 155mm Group became the Seacoast Artillery Group, and the 90mm outfit, with its searchlights, the Antiaircraft Artillery Group. No further changes took place before the battalion went overseas.

As this evolution in organization and weaponry began, Stephenson set to work building a segregated battalion with the African-American Marines available to him. They had undergone classification testing at Montford Point and been grouped according to their scores. Normally men in Category IV would at best attain the rank of corporal, whereas those in Categories III through I generally had the aptitude for higher

rank, though no black could aspire to officer training. Since classification scores tended to be fallible, Stephenson and his officers had to rely on instruction, observation, and evaluation as they tried to create a cadre of black noncommissioned officers in nine months or less.

Each group within the battalion—at the time 155mm artillery, 90mm antiaircraft artillery, and special weapons—maintained standing examination boards, which included the group commander. The officers and noncommissioned officers recommended candidates for promotion, who then appeared before the group's examining board. The first test in this series, for promotion to private first class, was a written examination usually administered during or shortly after boot camp, but the others, given during unit training, consisted of 25 to 30 questions answered orally. The names of those who survived the screening went to the battalion commander who matched candidates with openings. "Many qualified men waited from month to month," Stephenson recalled, although in six or eight instances over perhaps nine months "an especially meritorious, mature man was advanced two grades on successive days to place especially talented leaders in positions of responsibility." Just as "Hashmark" Johnson and Edgar Huff had advanced rapidly within the recruit training operation, Obie Hall became a platoon sergeant within six months of joining the battalion.

The tempo of training picked up throughout the summer and fall of 1943, as African-American noncommissioned officers replaced more of the white enlisted men who had taught them to handle weapons and lead men in combat. On 20 August, the 51st Defense Battalion suffered its first fatality. During a disembarkation exercise, while the Marines of the 155mm Artillery Group scrambled down a net draped over a

The creation of a cadre of African-American noncommissioned officers brought rapid promotion to those who had the abilities, as Edgar Huff, shown here as a first sergeant, the Marine Corps needed. Some especially meritorious mature men were advanced two grades on successive days to place talented leaders in positions of responsibility in field organizations.

wooden structure representing the side of a transport, Corporal Gilbert Fraser, Jr., slipped, fell into a landing craft in the water below, and suffered injuries that claimed his life. In memory of the 30-year-old graduate of Virginia Union College, the road leading from Montford Point Camp to the artillery range became Fraser Road.

Although the men of the 51st Defense Battalion had to assume the responsibilities of squad leaders and platoon sergeants even as they learned to care for and fire the battalion's weapons, the black Marines met this challenge, as they demonstrated in November 1943. During firing exercises—while Secretary of the Navy Knox, General Holcomb, and Colonel Johnson of the Selective Service System watched—an African-American crew opened fire with a 90mm gun at a sleeve target being towed overhead and hit it within just 60 seconds. Lieutenant Colonel Stephenson, listening for the Com-

mandant's reaction, heard him say "I think they're ready now." Few other crews in the 51st could match this performance, and a number of them clearly needed further training, as some of their officers warned at the time. The four days of firing at the end of November could not be repeated, however, for the unit would depart sooner than originally planned on the first leg of a journey to the Pacific.

Where in the Pacific area would that journey end? Marine Major General Charles F. B. Price, in command of American forces in Samoa, had already warned against sending the African-Americans there. He based his opinion on his interpretation of the science of genetics. The light-skinned Polynesians, whom he considered "primitively romantic" by nature, had mingled freely with whites to produce "a very high class half caste," and liaisons with Chinese had resulted in "a very desirable type" of offspring. The arrival of a battal-

ion of black Marines, however, would "infuse enough Negro blood into the population to make the island predominately Negro" and produce what Price considered "a very undesirable citizen." Better, the general suggested, to send the 51st Defense Battalion to a region populated by Melanesians, where the "higher type of intelligence" among the African-Americans would not only "cause no racial strain" but also "actually raise the level of physical and mental standards" among the black islanders. After the general forwarded his recommendation to Marine Corps headquarters, though not necessarily because of his reasoning, two black depot companies that arrived in Samoa during October 1943 were promptly sent elsewhere.

Whatever its ultimate destination, the 51st Defense Battalion started off to war early in January 1944, and by the 19th, most of the unit—less 400 men transferred to the newly organized 52d Defense Battalion—and

National Archives Photo 127-N-9007

A fall during an exercise comparable to this killed Cpl Gilbert Fraser, Jr., the first fatality suffered by the Montford Point Marines.

the bulk of its gear were moving by rail toward San Diego. On that day, while Stephenson supervised the loading of the last of the 175 freight cars assigned to move the unit's equipment, a few of the black Marines waiting to board a troop train began celebrating their imminent departure by downing a few beers too many at the Montford Point snack bar, which lived up to the nickname of "slop chute," universally applied to such facilities. The military police, all of them white, cut off the supply of beer by closing the place and forcing the blacks to leave. Once outside, the men of the battalion milled about and began throwing rocks and shattering the windows of the snack bar. Again the military police intervened, one of them firing shots into the air to disperse the unruly crowd. Some of the black Marines fled into the nearby theater, which the military police promptly shut down. At this point, someone fired 15 or 20 shots into the air from the vicinity of a footbridge linking

the Montford Point Camp with Camp Knox, the old CCC facility, where those members of the 51st still in the area had their quarters. A stray bullet wounded a drill instructor,

Corporal Rolland W. Curtiss, who was leading his platoon on a night march. Despite the injury and a momentary panic among his recruits, the corporal brought his men safely

A 90mm gun crew practices loading at Montford Point in preparatation for its deployment overseas to the Pacific and eventual combat operations in the war.

A gun crew of the 51st Defense Battalion trains for overseas deployment.

back to their barracks.

Although one rifle assigned to the battalion showed signs of firing and another appeared to have been cleaned with hair oil, perhaps to disguise recent use, neither could be linked to a specific Marine. Records proved to be in disarray, with serial numbers copied incorrectly and individuals in possession of weapons other than the ones they were supposed to have. The breakdown of accountability impeded a hurried investigation by Stephenson and four of his officers and prevented them from determining who had fired the shots.

The mix-up in weapons resulted from the confusion of the move and

the inexperience of recently promoted junior noncommissioned officers, who failed to ride herd on their men. Colonel Woods witnessed the results of this failure when he inspected the vacated quarters and found "a filthy and unsanitary area." Indeed, one of the noncoms later admitted to simply assuming that "someone is going to pick it up," much as parents would make sure that nothing of value remained behind when a family moved to a new house.

The failure in discipline that attended the departure of the 51st Defense Battalion from Montford Point led to the replacement of Lieutenant Colonel Stephenson, who had built the unit and earned the respect

of its men, by Colonel Curtis W. LeGette. The new commanding officer, a native of South Carolina and a Marine since 1910, had fought in France during World War I and been wounded at Blanc Mont in October 1918. His most recent assignment was as commanding officer of the 7th Defense Battalion in the Ellice Islands. Not only was LeGette replacing a popular commander, he got off to a bad start. In his first speech to the assembled battalion, he made the mistake of invoking the phrase "you people"—frequently used by officers when addressing their white units—but in this instance his choice of "you" instead of "we" convinced some of the African-Americans that their new commanding officer considered them outsiders rather than real Marines.

The 51st Defense Battalion at War

Because they were replacing the 7th Defense Battalion, LeGette's former command, already established in the Ellice group, the black Marines turned in all the heavy equipment they had brought with them from Montford Point and boarded the merchantman SS *Meteor*, which sailed from San Diego on 11 February 1944. Less than a month had elapsed since the last train left North Carolina on the first leg of the journey to war. While *Meteor* steamed toward the Ellice Islands, the 51st Defense Battalion divided into two components. Detachment A, led by Lieutenant Colonel Gould P. Groves, the executive officer, would garrison Nanomea Island, while the rest of the battalion, under Colonel LeGette, manned the defenses of Funafuti and nearby Nukufetau. By 27 February, the 51st completed the relief of the 7th Defense Battalion, taking over the white unit's weapons and equipment. One of the African-American Marines, upon first experiencing the isolation that surrounded him, suggested that the departing whites "were never so glad

The Death March

Fraser Road would figure in one of the legends of Montford Point, the so-called Death March. One of the black Marines living in the ramshackle barracks formerly occupied by the Civilian Conservation Corps grew bored and used his bayonet to punch a hole in a wall, which had all the durability of cardboard. The noncommissioned officers questioned the men, who refused to identify the person guilty of the vandalism. As a result, the sergeants staged a nighttime forced march—the Death March in the lore of the Montford Point Marines—but this failed to elicit the name they sought. According to one account, when the column reached the site of the brig on Fraser Road, the black Marines decided that to go further would dishonor the memory of a dead comrade, Corporal Gilbert Fraser, Jr., who was killed in a training accident. They broke ranks, rushed the brig, and demanded to be arrested—or so the legend states. Since the number of potential prisoners would have been far too many for the structure to accommodate—they were "hanging out the windows,"one of the black Marines has declared—the noncommissioned officers marched them back to the huts. Whatever the details, the incident became the source of pride and further intensified the solidarity among Montford Point's African-American Marines.

to see black people in their lives." A flurry of action briefly dispelled the feeling of loneliness. On 28 March, crews of the 155mm guns at Nanomea responded to the report of a prowling submarine by firing 11 rounds, but the Japanese craft, if actually present, escaped unscathed.

Colonel LeGette, who maintained his headquarters at Funafuti, received a letter from the Commandant of the Marine Corps calling attention to the poor condition of the trucks and weapons his battalion had left behind in California. This chilling message tended to confirm LeGette's reservations about the unit. His concerns focused on administrative procedures and the maintenance of equipment, activities that required close supervision by experienced noncommissioned officers, who were scarce in the unit. The battalion commander sought to fix the blame for the shortcomings that had been revealed and to correct them.

To fix responsibility, LeGette convened a board of investigation that condemned his predecessor for failing to whip the battalion into shape and recommended a trial by court-martial, but Stephenson responded with a spirited rejoinder that forestalled legal action. Most of the problems that troubled LeGette stemmed from something over which

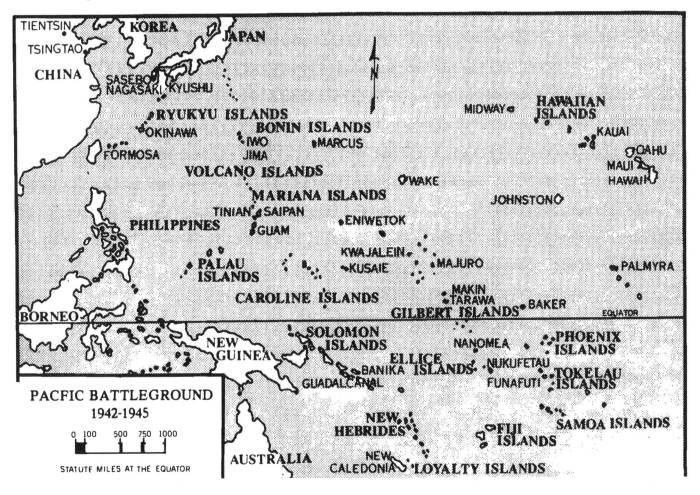

PACFIC BATTLEGROUND
1942-1945

0 100   500   750 1000

STATUTE MILES AT THE EQUATOR

The Route West

The 51st Defense Battalion's move across a segregated America began with a confrontation in Atlanta, Georgia, where one of the trains stopped so the men could have breakfast. Unaware of the layout of the Jim Crow railroad station, the noncommissioned officers moved the black Marines into a waiting room reserved for whites, only to be halted by white military police determined to uphold local law. The African-Americans stood ready to push their way through, but the train commander arrived, conferred with the officer in charge of the MPs, and prevented a tense situation from turning violent.

Elsewhere, the move to the West Coast went more smoothly. During a rest stop at Big Springs, Texas, one of the officers warned that this was Jim Crow country and urged the black Marines to be careful. They swarmed over the small town, however, and encountered no open hostility, obtaining service at the soda fountain or shooting pool at the facilities maintained for troops whose trains stopped at Big Springs. Further west, during a two-hour layover at Yuma, Arizona, Red Cross volunteers distributed candy, ice cream, fruit, magazines, and Bibles. One of the African-Americans, John R. Griffin, got the impression that "the entire city, including the Mexicans and Indians, came to the station to see the first Negro Defense Battalion go overseas."

At Camp Elliott, California, where the battalion made its final preparations for deployment to the Pacific, the racial climate more closely resembled Atlanta than Yuma or Big Springs. At an open-air movie, Jim Crow seating prevailed and the black Marines were ordered to the rear of the natural amphitheater that served as a theater. A spontaneous protest resulted in the expulsion of the men of the 51st, whose anger still boiled when they arrived at the battalion area. Stephenson tried to make up for the mistreatment of his Marines by liberally granting passes so they could find entertainment in nearby San Diego.

Stephenson had no control—the absence of a cadre of veteran black noncommissioned officers, itself the result of racial segregation and the exclusion of African-Americans from the prewar Marine Corps. Despite his successor's complaints, Stephenson considered the 51st Defense Battalion "the finest organization in the whole Negro program in the Marine Corps." Since the men of the unit did not know the details of the controversy involving the two commanders, morale remained high.

LeGette proposed a course of action to correct the flaws he had perceived. His remedy, however, included measures rendered impossible because of the demands of other units for officers and the policy of maintaining segregation in the enlisted force. He would have increased the number of white officers and warrant officers assigned to the unit and avoided the "occupational neurosis" resulting from service with blacks by replacing those officers who desired to leave the battalion. He further recommended the replacement of enlisted men in Categories IV and V with individuals who had scored better in the classification tests, a goal that could have been achieved only by raiding other black units.

The 51st Defense Battalion remained in the Ellice Islands roughly six months. When the black Marines received orders to depart, they carefully cleaned and checked the equipment inherited from the 7th Defense Battalion before turning everything over to the white 10th Defense Battalion. LeGette's unit set sail on 8 September 1944 for Eniwetok Atoll, a vast anchorage kept under sporadic surveillance, and occasionally harassed, by Japanese aircraft. The battalion stood ready to meet this threat from the skies, since it had reorganized two months earlier as an antiaircraft unit, losing its 155mm guns but adding a fourth 90mm battery and exchanging its machine guns and 20mm weapons for a second 40mm battery. The restructured unit kept its searchlights and radar. While the black Marines manned positions on four of the atoll's islands, Colonel LeGette on 13 December handed over the battalion to Lieutenant Colonel Groves. A member of the unit, Herman Darden, Jr., remembered that the departing commander "took us out on dress parade before he left, and stood there with tears in his eyes and told us . . . , 'You have shown me that you can soldier with the best of 'em.' "

The possibility of action lingered into 1945, kept alive by a report of marauding submarines and the possibility of aerial attack. One night, while the men of the 90mm antiaircraft group were watching a movie, the film abruptly stopped. Condition Red; Japanese aircraft were on the way. "I never saw such jubilation in my life," recalled Darden, for everyone responded eagerly. A Marine on a working party unloading ammunition might grumble about lifting a single 90mm round, but with combat seemingly minutes away, men "were running around with one under each arm." By dawn, the alert had ended; not even one Japanese aircraft tested the battalion's gun crews. "And from that high point on," Darden said, "the mental attitude seemed to dwindle."

Routine settled over Eniwetok, enveloping the unit that Groves now commanded. As one of its sergeants phrased it, "routine got boresome," punctuated only by the occasional crash or forced landing by American planes. A major change occurred on 12 June 1945, when the battalion commander formed a 251-man composite group, under Major William M. Tracy, for duty at Kwajalein

Atoll. Two days later, the group—consisting of a battery of 90mm guns, a 40mm platoon, and four searchlight sections—boarded an LST for the voyage. The contingent saw no combat at Kwajalein, nor did the remainder of the battalion at Eniwetok.

The 52d Defense Battalion

The second of the two African-American defense battalions took shape beginning on 15 December 1943 and rested firmly on a foundation supplied by the first. Colonel Augustus W. Cockrell, commanding officer of the 52d Defense Battalion, benefited from the cadre of 400 officers and men transferred from Colonel Stephenson's 51st Defense Battalion before it left Montford Point. These men, familiar with equipment and procedures after three

to six months with the 51st, enabled the 52d to avoid using on-the-job trainees as technicians and rapidly promoting men fresh from boot camp.

Like Woods, Stephenson, and LeGette, Cockrell was a Southerner, a native of Florida. He had enlisted in the Marines in 1918 and received a commission four years later. He had recently returned from the South Pacific, where he commanded the 2d and 8th Defense Battalions in Samoa and on Wallis Island. As time passed, Cockrell apparently won the affection of his noncommissioned officers, who respectfully called him "Old Gus," though not within his hearing.

In February 1944, the 52d Defense Battalion moved into the old CCC barracks at Camp Knox, which the last of Stephenson's men had just va-

cated. The 7th Separate Pack Howitzer Battery, organized originally as a component of the 51st Defense Battalion according to since-rescinded tables of organization, disbanded in March 1944, and the men joined Cockrell's command, providing another infusion of experience. A change to the tables of organization and equipment deprived the battalion in June 1944 of its seacoast artillery. Men from that component transferred to the Heavy Antiaircraft Group and formed a fourth 90mm battery. At the same time, the Light Antiaircraft Group (formerly the Special Weapons Group) substituted 40mm guns for its lighter weapons.

The command structure of both the battalion and the Montford Point Camp underwent change during July. Lieutenant Colonel Joseph W. Earnshaw, a native of Kansas and a graduate of the Naval Academy, arrived after duty at the Navy's Bureau of Ordnance in Washington, D.C., and took over the 52d Defense Battalion. Cockrell thereupon reported to camp headquarters as the designated replacement for Colonel Woods.

The first task that Earnshaw faced was a move to the Pacific Coast. The 52d Defense Battalion, instead of loading its heavy gear on trains as the 51st had done, turned in its trucks, antiaircraft guns, and other such equipment and divided into two groups. Earnshaw commanded one and entrusted the other to his executive officer, Lieutenant Colonel Thomas C. Moore, Jr., who hailed from Georgia and had commanded the 3d Defense Battalion on Guadalcanal in the Solomon Islands. The two contingents traveled on the same train to Camp Pendleton, California, to make final preparations for deployment to the islands of the Pacific.

The battalion arrived at Camp Pendleton on 24 August 1944, and on 21 September both components boarded the attack transport USS *Winged Arrow* (AP 170), which brought them to Pearl Harbor and

Black Marines practice climbing down a cargo net rigged in the swimming pool at Montford Point, developing an essential skill for amphibious warfare operations.
National Archives Photo 127-N-8275

"Hashmark" Johnson, shown posing with the mascot of the Montford Point Camp, became sergeant major of the 52d Defense Battalion on Guam in July 1945.

beaches, to the Marines fighting their way inland. To provide the missing segment of the supply line, the Marine Corps organized two kinds of units, depot companies and ammunition companies. Their comparatively compact size—companies rather than battalions—meant that the new organizations could be formed and trained rapidly and deployed in numbers that corresponded to the size of the amphibious forces being supported.

According to Edgar Huff, whose wartime assignments included first sergeant of a depot company, the new units consisted largely of recruits who had just returned from the rifle range. He conceded, however, that "all they needed was a strong back . . . to load and unload ships and haul ammunition to the line for the fighting troops"; further training might vary from a few weeks for the depot companies to a couple of months for the ammunition outfits. Black Marines assigned to the ammunition companies—in part, perhaps, because of the longer training and the danger inherent in handling explosives—tended to develop noticeably higher morale, along with sound discipline and a strong sense of purpose.

White officers led both kinds of units, with black noncommissioned officers ultimately taking over in the depot companies from first sergeant downward. In contrast, the ammunition companies had white noncommissioned officers down to the level of buck sergeant. The fuzes and shells handled by the ammunition companies required noncommissioned officers with technical knowledge and the ability to use this knowledge in enforcing safety rules, but in the midst of war the Marine Corps felt it did not have time to train inexperienced blacks for these duties and relied instead on previously trained whites. Because Marine Corps policy forbade a black platoon sergeant, for example, from giving orders to a junior noncommissioned officer who

thence to the Marshall Islands, where they took over from antiaircraft units already in place. One half of the divided battalion, the part that Moore led, landed at Majuro Atoll to protect Marine Aircraft Group 13 based there. The other, under Earnshaw, helped defend Roi and the adjacent island of Namur in Kwajalein Atoll, where Marine Aircraft Group 31 was located. For six months, October 1944 to March 1945, the battalion guarded against possible forays by increasingly feeble Japanese air power and, at Majuro, formed reconnaissance parties that boarded landing craft to search the smaller islands for Japanese and remove the natives from harm's way.

Lieutenant Colonel David W. Silvey, who had reported to Montford Point in May 1944 from the 6th Defense Battalion at Midway Island, replaced Earnshaw at Kwajalein on 10 January 1945. When the two halves of the battalion reunited on the recaptured island of Guam on 4 May 1945, Moore, who was senior to Silvey, assumed command. At Guam, the unit formed a part of the island's garrison.

Combat Service Support

By the spring of 1943, the Marine Corps discovered a need for full-time stevedores within the logistics system that channeled supplies from factories and warehouses in the United States, through rear area and forward support bases, over the

18

was white, the highest ranking African-American in an ammunition company could be only a buck sergeant, while the senior enlisted ranks remained exclusively white. The mess sergeant, who had no white cooks working for him, enjoyed the status of a staff noncommissioned officer, but he could not join the clubs available to whites of comparable rank, a source of annoyance to black enlisted men.

Although the Marine Corps envisioned these combat service support units as a source of labor, and the two defense battalions as combat outfits, wartime reality proved far different. The combat battalions fired not even a dozen rounds at what may have been a Japanese submarine, and their combat consisted of a few months of patrol action against surviving Japanese on the captured island of Guam. The depot and ammunition companies, however, saw savage fighting on the battlefields of Saipan, Tinian, Guam, Peleliu, Iwo Jima, and Okinawa. The combat service units suffered most of the casualties among African-American

Marines, who had seven of their number killed in action, two dead of wounds, 78 wounded in action, and nine victims of combat fatigue.

The 1st Marine Depot Company, the first of 51 such units, was activated on 8 March 1943 under Captain Jason M. Austin, Jr., assisted by two other officers. The initial enlisted complement consisted of nine white noncommissioned officers, who would serve only until blacks replaced them, 100 privates fresh from boot camp at Montford Point, and one African-American assistant cook, Ulysses J. Lucas, for a total of 110. Finding the necessary black noncommissioned officers proved so difficult that whites accompanied some of the depot companies overseas and remained with them until replacements became available, through either promotion or transfers from other black outfits.

The 1st Marine Ammunition Company was formed at Montford Point on 1 October 1943 under 2d Lieutenant Placido A. Gomez. This unit, as the 11 that followed, consisted of eight officers and 251 enlisted

men, the latter including specialists not available from the pool of black Marines at Montford Point, and had its own trucks, jeeps, and trailers for hauling ammunition. Because their job was considered more dangerous than the work of the depot companies, the ammunition companies trained for two months instead of three weeks. Some of the black noncommissioned officers underwent instruction in camouflage or the rudiments of ammunition handling, but only whites had the training or experience to fill the billets requiring higher-ranking technicians.

Although the organization of the ammunition companies remained essentially unchanged, the depot companies added a third platoon during the summer of 1943, increasing the aggregate strength to four officers and 162 enlisted men. In both types of units, the Marines carried rifles, carbines, or submachine guns, but had no mortars or machine guns. Between October 1943, when Lieutenant Gomez assumed command of the 1st Marine Ammunition Company, and September 1944, when the

The Marine Ammunition Companies and Marine Depot Companies helped deposit cargo on the beach, as at Iwo Jima, and move the supplies to the Marines fighting their way inland. They often were inserted into the front lines as riflemen.
Department of Defense Photo (USMC) 111947

12th and last of these units came into existence, Montford Point organized one ammunition company and two depot companies each month. The Marine Corps continued to form depot companies, with the last four—the 46th, 47th, 48th, and 49th—being organized in October 1945, a month after the war had ended. The anomaly in numbers, 51 companies but the highest number being the 49th Marine Depot Company, resulted from the organization of two 5th and two 6th Marine Depot Companies. The first pair went overseas in August 1943, provided reinforcements for previously deployed units so that each could add the authorized fourth platoon, and afterward disbanded.

Three weeks after its organization, the 1st Marine Depot Company boarded a train for the three-day journey to the West Coast. A veteran of a subsequent transcontinental deployment told of his company boarding a "sealed" train that stopped only for maintenance or emergencies. The Marines on board subsisted on rations loaded at Montford Point. Cars were crowded, toilets few, and showers non-existent. A fastidious few tried to take sponge baths. Everyone, however, had to shave every day or endure the consequences of the appearance of stubble: whatever number of push-ups a noncommissioned officer might demand.

The 1st Marine Depot Company arrived at San Diego on 5 April 1943, and according to the base newspaper, put on a "demonstration of close order drill that left observers gaping." On 16 April, the unit sailed for Noumea, New Caledonia, the initial destination of the first five depot companies dispatched to the Pacific. The organizations soon deployed to the Solomon and Russell Islands to support operations in the South Pacific and Central Pacific. The 2d and 4th Marine Ammunition Companies also arrived in the Solomons to prepare for future action.

Meanwhile, the Hawaiian Islands became a principal staging area for the thrust across the Central Pacific, and the 1st and 3d Marine Ammunition Companies went directly there. Also in Hawaii were five depot companies, including two that had spent nine months in Funafuti in the Ellice group, loading supplies destined for the fighting in the Gilbert and Marshall Islands, early objectives of the Central Pacific offensive. The combat support companies sent to the Hawaiian Islands arrived there in time to help load the ships that carried the 2d and 4th Marine Divisions to Saipan and to join the shore parties in unloading and distributing cargo at the objective.

Seizing the Mariana Islands Saipan, Tinian, and Guam

On D-Day, 15 June 1944, the depot companies saw action at Saipan, manhandling cargo from ships' holds into landing craft and finally distributing the supplies among the combat units. The 18th and 20th Marine Depot Companies landed with the 4th Marine Division on D-Day, while 19th company was going ashore with the 2d Marine Division. Attached to the 3d Battalion, 23d Marines, 4th Marine Division, one platoon of the 18th Company arrived at its assigned beach about two and one-half hours after the first wave. A mortar shell wounded four men of the depot company, who had to be evacuated for emergency treatment offshore, but the others kept moving inland. One squad fought as infantry to reinforce a thinly held line about a hundred yards from the water's edge. The next morning, the bulk of the company helped eliminate Japanese infiltrators who had penetrated along the boundary between the 23d Marines and the 8th Marines of the adjacent 2d Marine Division.

When the imediate threat had passed, the 18th Depot Company resumed its normal duties, "standing waist deep in surf unloading boats as vital supplies of food and water were brought in." In addition, said the unit commander, Captain William M. Barr, the black Marines "set up 'security' to keep out snipers as they helped load casualties aboard boats to go on hospital ships." In the face of intense fire, they "rode guard on trucks carrying high octane gasoline from the beach," and one squad leader killed a Japanese infiltrator who crept by night into a neighboring foxhole.

Another Marine Depot Company, the 20th, landed in the fourth wave in support of the 1st Battalion, 25th Marines, 4th Marine Division. In the words of Captain William C. Adams, the company commander, "all hell was breaking when we came in. It was still touch and go when we hit shore, and it took some time to establish a foothold." The captain's orderly, Private Kenneth J. Tibbs, suffered fatal wounds and died that very day, becoming the first African-American Marine killed in combat during the war. The remaining Marine depot company assigned to the operation, the 19th, supported the 2d Marine Division but did not come ashore until 22 June, one week after D-Day, and incurred no casualties.

During the D-Day landings at Saipan, while the depot companies underwent their baptism of fire, the 3d Marine Ammunition Company performed three closely related functions. As Sergeant Ernest W. Coney remembered that morning, some of the men helped move ammunition from ships into landing craft, and others worked on the pontoon barges, lashed to the sides of LSTs during the voyage from Hawaii and now moored on the ocean side of the reef, where they transferred the ammunition to DUKW amphibious trucks or LVT amphibian tractors for the final trip to shore. The rest of the company, Coney included, boarded landing craft to join the assault troops carving out a beachhead.

Since the boats could not cross the reef, the Marines shifted to amphibian tractors which clawed their way onto the beach at about 1400, as Japanese shells tore up the sand. "One team had an amphibian tractor shot out from under it as it was being unloaded," Coney reported, but "miraculously, all the men escaped without injury." Later that afternoon, Japanese fire cut down Private First Class Leroy Seals, who on the following day died of his wounds. On the night of 15 June, the black Marines of the ammunition company used their weapons to help beat back a Japanese counterattack, in the process silencing an enemy machine gun.

On Saipan, the black Leathernecks demonstrated they had earned the right to fight alongside their white fellow Marines. The accomplishments of the combat service support companies, reported the post newspaper at Camp Lejeune, so impressed the Commandant of the Marine Corps, Lieutenant General Alexander A. Vandegrift—who had replaced Holcomb on 1 January 1944—that he declared: "The Negro Marines are no longer on trial. They are Marines, period." *Time's* war correspondent in the Central Pacific, Robert Sherrod, wrote: "The Negro Marines, under fire for the first time, have rated a universal 4.0 on Saipan." In other words, they had earned the Navy's highest possible rating.

At another of the Mariana Islands, Guam, which lay southwest of Saipan, amphibious forces attempted to regain American territory seized by the Japanese in December 1941. On 21 July 1944, three days before the landing at Tinian, three platoons of the 2d Marine Ammunition Company supported the 3d Marine Division as it stormed the northern beaches, while the 4th Ammunition Company and one platoon of the 2d assisted the 1st Provisional Marine Brigade at the southern beachhead. The black Marines with the 3d Marine Division suffered one man wounded and no one killed, even though the Japanese laid down in-

On Saipan, where black Marines earned praise from the Commandant of the Marine Corps, LtGen Alexander A. Van- *degrift, four members of the 3d Marine Ammunition Company pose with a Japanese bicycle they captured.*
Department of Defense Photo (USMC) 86008

Mop-up on Guam

Although officially secure, Guam still teemed with thousands of Japanese, bypassed in the lightning campaign during July and August 1944, who opened fire from ambush and lashed out against rear area installations from the concealment of the jungle. Private First Class Luther Woodward of the 4th Marine Ammunition Company displayed a gift for tracking enemy stragglers. One afternoon, he came across fresh footprints near the ammunition dump and followed them to a hut where a half-dozen Japanese had taken refuge. He opened fire, killing one, wounding another, and scattering the rest. Woodward returned to the camp, got five other black Marines to join him, and hunted down the survivors. He killed one of them, and his companions killed another. This exploit earned him a Bronze Star for heroism, later upgraded to the more prestigious Silver Star.

Some Japanese stragglers still held out in March 1945 when Lieutenant Colonel Thomas C. Moore, Jr., arrived at Guam with the portion of the 52d Defense Battalion that had helped defend Majuro. The newcomers promptly clashed with the Japanese, who found concealment in dense vegetation that one of the black Marines said was "as thick as the hair on a dog's back." The patrols dispatched to secure the approaches to the battalion's camp could number no more than ten men, for larger groups lost cohesion in the jungle undergrowth. On 1 April, Sergeant Ezra Kelly killed one of two Japanese discovered within a thousand yards of the camp. Subsequent probes of the jungle during April killed two more Japanese and wounded four others, but on the 26th enemy fire wounded one of the Marines, Private First Class Ernest J. Calland.

During the summer of 1945, the 52d Defense Battalion — the rest of the unit had reached Guam early in May — prepared to deploy to Okinawa, where aircraft based in Japan still posed a threat. Loading had already begun when, on 9 July, orders were changed; the unit would remain on Guam. According to Private First Class John Griffin, "morale dropped 99 percent. for the next week or ten days the men stayed around their tents writing letters and what not. Instead of being a Defense Unit, we turned out to be nothing more than a working battalion." The procession of trucks roaring into the area to take working parties to the harbor startled "Hashmark" Johnson, taking over as sergeant major of what he thought was a combat unit. He persuaded Lieutenant Colonel Moore to resume aggressive patrolling, as much to restore unit morale as to eliminate the die-hard Japanese. During this activity, Ezra Kelly added to his toll, killing a total of six Japanese on Guam; he received promotion to platoon sergeant, and earned high marks from Johnson, who described him as "really gung ho. Absolutely fearless." Like Kelly, Johnson led patrols into the boondocks and set up successful ambushes.

tense fire from the high ground overlooking the invasion site. In the south, the reinforced 4th Marine Ammunition Company set up the brigade ammunition dump and dug in to protect it throughout the night of D-Day. Under cover of darkness, the enemy tried to blow up the dump, but the African-American Marines killed 14 explosives-laden infiltrators at no loss to themselves. The ammunition and depot companies were still supporting the assault forces on 10 August, when the objective was declared secure. The Navy Unit Commendation awarded the 1st Provisional Marine Brigade included the black Marines of the 4th Marine Ammunition Company and the attached platoon from the 2d Company.

The final objective of the Marianas campaign was Tinian. African-American Marines who had seen action on Saipan boarded landing craft there and proceeded directly to the nearby island. Elements of the 3d Marine Ammunition Company joined the assault troops of the 4th Marine Division on 24 July, and the depot companies followed up in support of that organization and the 2d Marine Division, which landed on the 26th. Because of the performance of the black Marines on Saipan and Tinian, the 3d Marine Ammunition Company and the 18th, 19th, and 20th Marine Depot Companies, components of the 7th Field Depot, shared in the Presidential Unit Citation awarded the 4th Marine Division.

Peleliu and Iwo Jima

When the 1st Marine Division, on 15 September 1944, attacked the heavily defended island of Peleliu in the Palau group, the 16th Field Depot supported the assault troops. The field depot included two African-American units, the 11th Marine Depot Company and the 7th Marine Ammunition Company. The 11th Marine Depot Company responded beyond the call of duty and paid the price, 17 wounded, the highest casualty rate of any company of African-American Marines during the entire war. Major General William H. Rupertus, who commanded the 1st Marine Division, sent identical letters of commendation to the commanders of both companies, praising the black Marines for their "whole hearted cooperation and untiring efforts" which "demonstrated in every respect" that they "appreciate the privilege of wearing a Marine uniform and serving with Marines in combat."

Black combat support units also took part in the assault on Iwo Jima, where, as at Peleliu, their presence confounded the policy of segregation. Because of the random intermingling of white and black units, an African-American Marine, carrying a box of supplies, dived into a shell hole occupied by white Marines, one of whom gave him a cigarette before he scrambled out with his load and ran forward. Here, too, black stewards and members of the depot and ammunition companies came to the aid of the wounded. A white Marine, Robert F. Graf, who lay in a tent awaiting evacuation for further medical treatment, remembered that:

"Two black Marines . . . ever so gently . . . placed me on a stretcher and carried me outside to a waiting DUKW."

At Iwo Jima, the 8th Marine Ammunition Company and the 33d, 34th, and 36th Marine Depot Companies served as part of the shore party of the V Amphibious Corps. Elements of the ammunition company and the 36th Depot Company landed on D-Day, 19 February 1945, and within three days all the units

were ashore, braving Japanese fire as they struggled in the volcanic sand to unload and stockpile ammunition and other supplies, and move the cargo inland. Eleven black enlisted Marines and one of the white officers were wounded, two of the enlisted men fatally.

The depot companies landed cargo attached by steel straps to wooden pallets to simplify stowage in cargo holds and unloading at the objective. Unfortunately, the black Marines

The Third Battle of Guam

Some six months after the invasion of the Mariana Islands, violence shook the conquered island of Guam for the third time in the course of the war. The first battle of Guam took place on 10 December 1941, when the Japanese overwhelmed the almost defenseless American possession. During the second, Marines and Army troops landed on 21 July 1944 and recaptured the island. The third battle erupted in December 1944 between Americans, black and white, and culminated in a riot on Christmas night.

This third battle began with an attempt by whites of the 3d Marine Division, some of them replacements new to the unit, to prevent blacks, most of them sailors, from visiting the town of Agana and the women who lived there. A black Marine stationed on the island compared Guam to "a city deep down in the South" because of the hostility he encountered. "But as we all know," he explained, "where there are women and white and Negro men, you will find discrimination in large quantities." On Guam, discrimination against blacks involved attempted intimidation by whites who shouted insults, threw rocks, and occasionally hurled smoke grenades from passing trucks into the cantonment area for black sailors of the Naval Supply Depot.

By mid-December, the island's Provost Marshal, Marine Colonel Benjamin A. Atkinson, considered the situation so dangerous that he urged his commander, Major General Henry L. Larsen, to take action. Larsen, whose casual remarks at Montford Point, including the reference to "you people in our uniform," had become a legend among the black Marines, responded with an order that sought to unite the races. Using carefully chosen words, the general wrote that:

The present war has called together in our services men of many origins and various races and colors. All are presumed to be imbued with common ideals and standards. All wear the uniform of the United States. All are entitled to the respect to which that common service is entitled. There shall be no dis-

crimination by reason of sectional birth, race, religion, or political beliefs. On the other hand, all individuals are charged with the responsibility of conducting themselves as becomes Americans.

Larsen believed in the principles he thus enunciated and, as a subsequent investigation concluded, intended to put them into effect, but his words came too late. In a series of violent incidents, an off-duty white military policeman fired at some blacks in Agana but hit no one; a white sailor shot to death a black Marine of the 25th Depot Company in a quarrel over a woman; and a sentry from the 27th Marine Depot Company reacted to harassment by fatally wounding his tormentor, a white Marine. Courts-martial eventually convicted the men who fired the fatal shots of voluntary manslaughter, but before justice could prevail, a misunderstanding led to a race riot.

A rumor that the black victim had been a sailor killed by a white Marine, spread unchallenged among the African-Americans of the Naval Supply Depot. Some of them commandeered two trucks and drove into Agana seeking revenge, but Marine military police succeeded in defusing the situation. On Christmas night, however, 43 black sailors armed themselves with knives and clubs and invaded a camp that housed white Marines. The ensuing riot resulted in the arrest of the black sailors who carried out the attack.

General Larsen convened a court of inquiry, which took testimony for an entire month. As president, he selected Colonel Woods, the former commanding officer at Montford Point, who happened to be serving on Guam. Walter White, Secretary of the National Association for the Advancement of Colored People, was on a fact-finding tour of the Pacific theater and participated in the proceedings. His piecing together of a pattern of pervasive racial harassment—unofficial, spontaneous, but nonetheless cruel—may have helped bring about convictions, not of the black rioters alone, but also of some of the whites who tormented them.

Black Marines pose with one of the Army DUKW amphibious trucks used to bring cargo ashore and carry away the wounded for medical treatment to ships offshore.

had no tools, like bolt-cutters, that could easily sever the metal. An officer of one of the companies recalls that his men had to break the straps by hacking and twisting with their bayonets.

The hard-fought advance inland eased the pressure on rear-area installations but did not eliminate the danger to combat service support troops like the men of the 8th Marine Ammunition Company. On 1 March, for example, Japanese mortar shells started a fire in the ammunition dump operated by the company, but Second Lieutenant John D'Angelo and several black Marines, among them Corporal Ralph Balara, shoveled sand onto the flames and extinguished them. During darkness on the following morning, another enemy barrage struck the dump, this time detonating a bunker filled with high-explosive and white-phosphorous shells. The exploding ammunition started fires throughout the dump, generating heat so intense that it forced D'Angelo and his platoon to fall back and warped the steel barrel of a carbine they left behind. Not until the conflagration had burned it-

self out, could the platoon begin the dangerous job of extinguishing the embers and salvaging any usable ammunition. Sergeant Tom McPhatter —an African-American noncommissioned officer, who after the war became a clergyman and a Navy chaplain, attaining the rank of captain—helped search the ruins of the dump. On 4 March, D'Angelo's platoon braved sniper fire at a captured airfield to retrieve an emergency load of ammunition dropped by parachute to replace what the blaze had consumed.

On the early morning of 26 March, 10 days after Iwo Jima was declared secure, the Japanese made a final attack that penetrated to the rear area units near Iwo Jima's western beaches, including the 8th Ammunition and 36th Marine Depot Companies. The black Marines helped stop the enemy in a confused struggle during darkness and mop up the survivors at daybreak. Two members of the 36th Company—Privates James M. Whitlock and James Davis —earned the Bronze Star for "heroic achievement." One Marine from the depot company and another from the

ammunition company were fatally wounded, but four others, two from each unit, survived their wounds. The African-American companies that fought at Iwo Jima shared in the Navy Unit Citation awarded the support units of V Amphibious Corps.

Okinawa, Japan, and China

The fight for Okinawa, which proved to be the last battle of World War II, involved some 2,000 black Marines, a larger concentration than for any previous operation. On 1 April 1945, the 6th and 1st Marine Divisions stormed ashore alongside two Army divisions, while the 2d Marine Division engaged in a feint to pin down the island's Japanese defenders. The three ammunition and four depot companies assigned to the 7th Field Depot, supporting the III Marine Amphibious Corps on that day, were divided between the demonstration and assault forces. The 1st and 3d Ammunition Companies and the 5th, 38th, and part of the 37th Marine Depot Companies accompanied the 2d Marine Division, while the 12th Ammunition and 18th Depot Companies, along with the rest of the 37th, participated in the landings by the 1st and 6th Marine Divisions. Within three days, almost all of the amphibious force's black Marines were in action ashore, and reinforcements soon arrived. By the end of April, the 20th Marine Depot Company reached Okinawa from Saipan, and in May the 9th and 10th Depot Companies from Guadalcanal, together with the 19th from Saipan, joined the 7th Field Depot.

Drenching rain and seemingly bottomless mud hampered the work of the ammunition and depot companies as the troops advanced and supply lines grew longer. The same parties that moved ammunition and other cargo forward to sustain the fighting also brought back the wounded. Stewards, too, made an essential contribution to eventual victory by serving as stretcher bearers.

On the beach at Iwo Jima, two black Marines crawl past the smouldering hulk of a DUKW all the while being subjected to heavy Japanese machine gun, mortar, and artillery fire. They struggled in the volcanic sand to set up supply dumps.

Indeed, casualties were almost equally divided between combat service units, 11 wounded, and the Stewards' Branch, seven wounded, one of them twice, and one killed.

The exhausting work of handling supplies continued after Okinawa was declared secure on 22 June 1945, for the island became a base from which to invade Japan. When hostilities ended on 15 August, after the dropping of atomic bombs on Hiroshima and Nagasaki, the III Marine Amphibious Corps received orders to proceed to North China. Meanwhile, the V Amphibious Corps, which had conquered Iwo Jima, would participate in the occupation of Japan.

Assigned to the 8th Service Regiment (formerly the 8th Field Depot) in support of the Marine V Amphibious Corps, the 6th, 8th, and 10th Ammunition Companies arrived in conquered Japan between 22 and 26 September, along with the 24th, 33d, 34th, 42d, and 43d Depot Companies. The 36th Marine Depot Company joined the earlier arrivals by the end of October. Even though the mingling of Marine units on the battlefields of the Pacific War had broken down, at least temporarily, the wall separating blacks from whites, the occupation forces in Japan—and in North China, as well—reestablished racial segregation.

The African-American Marines who landed in North China at the end of September 1945—men of the 1st and 12th Ammunition Companies and the 5th, 20th, 37th, and 38th Depot Companies—encountered a cool initial reception from the Chinese. Edgar Huff recalled that a

PFCs Willie J. Kanady, Eugene F. Hill, and Joe Alexander of the 34th Depot Company relax during a lull in the action on Iwo Jima, where danger persisted even after the island was declared secure. Before they left Iwo, the company would become engaged when the Japanese mounted a banzai charge against Marines and soldiers.

Men of the 12th Marine Ammunition Company pose at a monument overrun during the Okinawa campaign, in which some 2,000 black Marines participated.

Chinese might run up to a black Marine and touch his face, as if to determine if the color would rub off on the fingers. Until the sight of African-Americans became familiar, the local civilians remained wary of them, but, Huff continued, "as soon as they found that this paint wouldn't come off, or what they thought was paint," the Chinese "got to be very charming and very lovely." Because local labor proved readily available, the men of the depot and ammunition companies frequently performed guard duty at American installations and on the trains that Communist guerrilla forces preyed upon in their war against the Nationalist govern-

ment, which was trying to assert its authority in the region.

Returning Home

Hostilities against Japan ended on 15 August 1945, and four days later, the 52d Defense Battalion at Guam began a transition from combat unit to support organization. The change received official confirmation on 30 September when the battalion came under the 5th Service Depot, which also controlled the black ammunition and depot companies still on the island. A detachment from the 52d sailed to the Marshalls in October, relieved the 51st Defense Battalion at Eniwetok and Kwajalein, and re-

turned to Guam in January. Some of the Marines not yet eligible for discharge cast off the role of depot troops and formed the Heavy Antiaircraft Group (Provisional), based at Saipan until disbanded in February 1947. The Marines of the 52d Defense Battalion, who remained on Guam after the group departed for Saipan, sailed for San Diego in the transport USS *Wakefield* (AP 21) on 13 March 1946. As a rule, the Marine Corps discharged on the West Coast the men with homes west of the Mississippi River, while those living to the east of the river received their discharges on the East Coast. The men of the 52d Defense Battalion not discharged at Camp Pendleton returned to Montford Point, where Lieutenant Colonel Moore relinquished command on 21 April. The end came on 15 May when the wartime unit was redesignated the 3d Antiaircraft Artillery Battalion in the postwar Marine Corps.

After the unit's relief in November 1945 by African-American Marines from the 52d Defense Battalion, the bulk of the 51st Defense Battalion sailed from Eniwetok to San Diego and then went to Camp Pendleton, California, where some of the men with long service overseas received their discharges. The members of the Eniwetok detachment not yet discharged traveled by train to Montford Point where they met the Kwajalein group, which had arrived by sea at Norfolk. On 31 January 1946, the first African-American combat unit organized by the Marine Corps for service in World War II officially disbanded.

Along with the two defense battalions, the ammunition and depot units headed home from the Pacific and the Far East. Scarcely had the African-American combat service companies arrived in Japan for occupation duty when they became part of the postwar demobilization, either disbanding in place, transferring to Guam, or, in the case of the

Unfinished Business

Although African-American enlisted men earned acceptance on the battlefields of the war against Japan, the Marine Corps did not commission even one black officer in the course of the conflict. The black press showed enthusiasm from the outset for the men of Montford Point, but complained about the absence of African-American officers. "18,000 colored Marines," editorialized the *Baltimore Afro-American*, "but not one colored officer." At last, early in 1945, three senior black noncommissioned officers entered officer training at Quantico, Virginia, but not even one graduated, a failure rate that, in the words of "Hashmark" Johnson, raised "a number of questions" among Montford Point Marines and caused "quite a bit of consternation." These concerns may well have been justified, since all three of the men went on to successful careers as civilians: Sergeant Major Charles F. Anderson as an attorney; Sergeant Major Charles W. Simmons as a college professor and author; and First Sergeant George F. Ellis, Jr., as a physician. Three more African-American officer candidates failed to win commissions, and not until 10 November 1945, the birthday of the Marines, did the Corps commission the first black officer in its history. On that day, Frederick C. Branch, a veteran of the 51st Defense Battalion, became a Second Lieutenant in the Reserve.

Unlike the Army and Navy, the Marine Corps barred blacks from its wartime Women Reserves. In adopting this ban, it could cite the expense of building segregated quarters and the fact that enough white applicants were available to maintain the organization at authorized strength. The first African-American to join the Women Reserves, Annie E. Graham, did not enlist until September 1949, four years after Japan's formal surrender.

21 February at Montford Point. On 2 March, the other African-American units sent to North China sailed eastward across the Pacific. The 12th Marine Ammunition Company paused at Pearl Harbor to transfer to the 6th Service Depot those men not yet eligible for discharge. The company's veterans, however, arrived at Montford Point in time for their unit to disband on 5 April, three days after the 37th and 38th Depot Companies had ceased to exist.

The 6th Service Depot (originally the 6th Base Depot) had functioned in Hawaii throughout the Central Pacific offensive, and since 1944 it included a succession of ammunition and depot companies manned by African-American Marines. While the fighting raged, the men of these units had worked 12-hour shifts to channel supplies to the Marines closing in on Japan. The coming of peace changed all that. By mid-summer 1946, only the 47th Marine Depot Company and one platoon of the

10th Marine Ammunition Company, returning by way of San Diego to Montford Point and disbanding there. Except for a few stewards, the last black Marines left Japan in April 1946.

As part of the reduction of Marine Corps strength in Japan, the 8th Marine Ammunition Company and 33d, 34th, and 36th Marine Depot Companies joined the 5th Service Depot (formerly the 5th Field Depot) at Guam, where other African-American Marine units already served. The disbanding of the black units on Guam began on 31 October 1945 with the 4th Depot Company and ended with the 8th Ammunition Company and 49th Depot Company on 30 September 1947.

The postwar reduction of strength affected the black units in North China, as it did those in Japan. The 5th and 20th Depot and 1st Ammunition Companies left China in January 1946, passed through San Diego and Camp Pendleton, and disbanded on

On 10 November 1945, Frederick C. Branch, the first African-American ever commissioned in the Marine Corps, and a veteran of the 51st Defense Battalion, smiles proudly as his wife pins the gold bars of a second lieutenant on his uniform.
Department of Defense Photo (USMC) 500043

Guam-based 8th Ammunition Company remained on the island of Oahu. The depot outfit disbanded on 31 October 1946, and in November, the platoon sailed to Guam, where its was absorbed into its parent company, which disbanded at the end of September 1947.

Pride Mixed with Bitterness

Of the 19,168 African-Americans who served in the Marine Corps during World War II, 12,738 went overseas in the defense battalions or combat support companies or as stewards. Those who remained in the United States performed numerous duties: stewards in officers' messes at various headquarters; staff members at the Montford Point Camp or recruits in training there when the conflict ended; or service troops at supply depots at Philadelphia or Norfolk or the Naval Ammunition Depot at McAlester, Oklahoma.

While the African-American Marines in the United States braved loneliness and racial discrimination, those overseas might wait on distant islands for Japanese attacks that never came; manhandle heavy containers out of ships' holds; load all sorts of supplies into landing craft; sort out the cargo on the beachhead, often under deadly fire; and move the desperately need material inland to the fighting units. Men in the defense battalions sometimes unloaded ships, whereas members of the combat support companies became infantrymen in an emergency, and stewards often doubled as stretcher bearers. Looking back at a succession of exhausting, dangerous, and at times boring assignments with the 3d Marine Ammunition Company, Robert D. Little said: "If I had to do it all over again, I'd still be a black Marine . . . . I think they made a man of me."

Brooks E. Gray, who helped form the Montford Point Marine Association to preserve the heritage of the wartime black Marines, has spoken of the "pride mixed with bitterness" experienced by the African-Americans who wore the uniform of the Marine Corps during World War II. Segregation prevailed at the time, even following the black Marines across the Pacific to Japan and the Asian mainland. "The injustices . . . in those segregated units," Gray recalled, "sparked a fierce determination to excel." And these African-Americans did excel. "We represented," he believed, "the breakthrough of the final barrier"—the obstacle of racism —"by being part of the elite corps." Events proved Gray correct, for the post-World War II Marine Corps could never return to the racial policy of 1940. Blacks had won the fight for the right to serve; they were in the Marine Corps to stay. Moreover, integration of the races would come to the Corps, though that radical change had to await President Harry S. Truman's executive order banning racial discrimination in the armed forces, issued in 1948, and the demands for manpower imposed by the Korean War, which broke out two years later. By the time Gray retired in 1969 as a master gunnery sergeant after 24 years of service, the Marine Corps had committed itself to racial integration.

BLACK MARINE UNITS
OF THE FLEET MARINE FORCE, WORLD WAR II

Date of Activation	Unit Designation	Date of Deactivation	Where Deactivated
18 Aug 1942	51st Composite Def Bn	31 Jan 1946	Montford Point
8 Mar 1943	1st Marine Depot Co	4 Jan 1946	Montford Point
23 Apr 1943	2d Marine Depot Co	4 Jan 1946	Montford Point
23 Apr 1943	3d Marine Depot Co	4 Jan 1946	Montford Point
1 June 1943	4th Marine Depot Co	31 Oct 1945	Guam
8 Jul 1943	5th Marine Depot Co	31 Oct 1943	New Caledonia
8 Jul 1943	6th Marine Depot Co	31 Aug 1943	New Caledonia
16 Aug 1943	7th Marine Depot Co	11 Dec 1945	Montford Point
16 Aug 1943	8th Marine Depot Co	10 Dec 1945	Montford Point
15 Sep 1943	9th Marine Depot Co	31 Dec 1945	Montford Point
15 Sep 1943	10th Marine Depot Co	22 Dec 1945	Montford Point
1 Oct 1943	1st Marine Ammunition Co	21 Feb 1946	Montford Point
7 Oct 1943	11th Marine Depot Co	4 Dec 1945	Saipan
7 Oct 1943	12th Marine Depot Co	11 Dec 1945	Montford Point
1 Nov 1943	13th Marine Depot Co	30 Nov 1945	Guam
1 Nov 1943	14th Marine Depot Co	30 Nov 1945	Guam
1 Nov 1943	2d Marine Ammunition Co	20 Jan 1946	Guam
1 Dec 1943	15th Marine Depot Co	30 Nov 1945	Allen Island
2 Dec 1943	16th Marine Depot Co	29 Jan 1946	Montford Point
2 Dec 1943	3d Marine Ammunition Co	25 Feb 1946	Montford Point
15 Dec 1943	52d Defense Bn	14 May 1946	Montford Point
1 Jan 1944	17th Marine Depot Co	16 Jan 1946	Montford Point
1 Jan 1944	18th Marine Depot Co	29 Jan 1946	Montford Point
1 Jan 1944	4th Marine Ammunition Co	8 Mar 1946	Guam
1 Feb 1944	19th Marine Depot Co	25 Feb 1946	Montford Point
1 Feb 1944	20th Marine Depot Co	21 Feb 1946	Montford Point
1 Feb 1944	5th Marine Ammunition Co	4 Jul 1946	Montford Point
1 Mar 1944	21st Marine Depot Co	2 Apr 1946	Montford Point
1 Mar 1944	22d Marine Depot Co	2 Apr 1946	Montford Point
1 Mar 1944	6th Ammunition Co	15 Dec 1945	Sasebo
1 Apr 1944	23d Marine Depot Co	5 Apr 1946	Montford Point
1 Apr 1944	24th Marine Depot Co	15 Nov 1945	Nagasaki
1 Apr 1944	7th Marine Ammunition Co	8 May 1946	Montford Point
1 May 1944	25th Marine Depot Co	2 May 1946	Montford Point
1 May 1944	26th Marine Depot Co	2 May 1946	Montford Point
1 May 1944	8th Marine Ammunition Co	30 Sep 1947	Guam
1 Jun 1944	27th Marine Depot Co	16 Apr 1946	Montford Point
1 Jun 1944	28th Marine Depot Co	2 May 1946	Montford Point
1 Jun 1944	9th Marine Ammunition Co	4 Jul 1946	Montford Point
1 Jul 1944	29th Marine Depot Co	8 May 1946	Montford Point
1 Jul 1944	30th Marine Depot Co	8 Apr 1946	Montford Point
1 Jul 1944	10th Marine Ammunition Co	6 May 1946	Montford Point
1 Aug 1944	31st Marine Depot Co	30 Nov 1945	Maui
1 Aug 1944	32d Marine Depot Co	8 May 1946	Montford Point
1 Aug 1944	11th Marine Ammunition Co	4 Jul 1946	Montford Point
1 Sep 1944	33d Marine Depot Co	31 Jan 1946	Guam
1 Sep 1944	34th Marine Depot Co	31 Jan 1946	Guam
1 Sep 1944	12th Marine Ammunition Co	5 Apr 1946	Montford Point
1 Oct 1944	35th Marine Depot Co	6 Jun 1946	Montford Point
1 Oct 1944	36th Marine Depot Co	17 Jun 1946	Montford Point
1 Nov 1944	37th Marine Depot Co	2 Apr 1946	Montford Point
1 Nov 1944	38th Marine Depot Co	2 Apr 1946	Montford Point
1 Nov 1944	5th Marine Depot Co	21 Feb 1946	Montford Point
1 Dec 1944	6th Marine Depot Co	31 Dec 1945	Guam
1 Dec 1944	39th Marine Depot Co	10 Jun 1946	Guam
1 Dec 1944	40th Marine Depot Co	4 May 1946	Saipan
3 Mar 1945	41st Marine Depot Co	23 Mar 1946	Maui
14 Mar 1945	42d Marine Depot Co	15 Mar 1946	Sasebo
14 Mar 1945	43d Marine Depot Co	15 Mar 1946	Sasebo
18 Apr 1945	44th Marine Depot Co	8 May 1946	Montford Point
10 Aug 1945	45th Marine Depot Co	6 Jun 1946	Montford Point
1 Oct 1945	46th Marine Depot Co	15 Jul 1946	Montford Point
1 Oct 1945	47th Marine Depot Co	31 Oct 1946	Oahu
1 Oct 1945	48th Marine Depot Co	10 Jun 1946	Guam
1 Oct 1945	49th Marine Depot Co	30 Sep 1947	Guam

Sources

Three books contain narratives of varying lengths that recount the history of African-American Marines in World War II. Perry E. Fisher and Brooks E. Gray, veterans of the 8th Marine Ammunition Company, have written *Blacks and Whites Together Through Hell: U.S. Marines in World War II* (Turlock, California: Millsmont Publishing, 1993). In his *Defense Studies: Integration of the Armed Forces, 1940-1965* (Washington: Center of Military History, 1981), Morris J. MacGregor, Jr., devotes part of one chapter to the black Marines of World War II. The most detailed account of the Montford Point Marines may be found in Henry I. Shaw, Jr., and Ralph W. Donnelly's *Blacks in the Marine Corps* (Washington: History and Museums Division, Headquarters U. S. Marine Corps, 1975, reprinted 1988).

Many of the directives, memoranda, and reports dealing with the topic of African-Americans in the Marine Corps during World War II appear in Volume 6 of *Blacks in the United States Armed Forces: Basic Documents* (Wilmington, Delaware: Scholarly Resources, 1977), edited by Morris J. MacGregor, Jr., and Bernard C. Nalty.

The Marine Corps Oral History Collection includes a number of interviews that deal with the recruitment, training, and employment of African-American Marines during World War II, grouped together under the title "Black Marines." The Marine Corps Personal Papers collection includes accounts of wartime service by black veterans.

Henry I. Shaw, Jr., co-author of *Blacks in the Marine Corps*, commented on this manuscript, as did Joseph H. Carpenter, who is National Historian of the Montford Point Marine Association.

About the Author

Bernard C. Nalty, a civilian member of the Marine Corps history program from October 1956 to September 1961, collaborated with Henry I. Shaw, Jr. and Edwin T. Turnbladh on *Central Pacific Drive*, volume three of *History of Marine Corps Operations in World War II*. Together with Morris J. MacGregor, he edited the 13-volume series *Blacks in the United States Armed Forces: Basic Documents* and its one-volume abridgement, *Blacks in the Military: Essential Documents*. His other works include *Strength for the Fight: A History of Black Americans in the Military*.

ERRATA

In the pamphlet *Closing In: Marines in the Seizure of Iwo Jima*, in this series, two Marine units are incorrectly identified. On page 31, the correct reference is "Captain Thomas M. Fields, commanding officer of Company D, 2d Battalion, 26th Marines . . . ." On page 36, it is "Captain Frank C. Caldwell, commanding Company F, 2d Battalion, 26th Marines . . . ." In *Breaching the Marianas: The Battle for Saipan*, GySgt Robert H. McCard, 4th Tank Battalion, 4th Marine Division, was inadvertently omitted from the list of recipients of the Medal of Honor. In *Free a Marine to Fight: Women Marines in World War II*, the photo caption on page 18 should read: "Pvt Billie J. Redding married her hometown beau, Navy Ens William A. Lewis, in a military wedding in San Diego. In order not to violate uniform regulations, both the bride and her maid of honor, Helen Taylor, carried rather than wore their corsages."

WORLD WAR II

THIS PAMPHLET HISTORY, one in a series devoted to U.S. Marines in the World War II era, is published for the education and training of Marines by the History and Museums Division, Headquarters, U.S. Marine Corps, Washington, D.C., as a part of the U.S. Department of Defense observance of the 50th anniversary of victory in that war.

Editorial costs of preparing this pamphlet have been defrayed in part by a grant from the Marine Corps Historical Foundation.

WORLD WAR II COMMEMORATIVE SERIES

DIRECTOR OF MARINE CORPS HISTORY AND MUSEUMS
Brigadier General Edwin H. Simmons, USMC (Ret)

GENERAL EDITOR,
WORLD WAR II COMMEMORATIVE SERIES
Benis M. Frank

CARTOGRAPHIC CONSULTANT
George C. MacGillivray

EDITING AND DESIGN SECTION, HISTORY AND MUSEUMS DIVISION
Robert E. Struder, Senior Editor; **W. Stephen Hill,** Visual Information Specialist
Catherine A. Kerns, Composition Services Technician

Marine Corps Historical Center

Building 58, Washington Navy Yard
Washington, D.C. 20374-5040

1995
PCN 190 003132 00

Blacks in WWII
My War Too

We need YOUR help. Please do the following.

1. Like us on Facebook:

Blacks in WWII—My War Too

And share the page with others

2. Purchase our Products.

11X17 Poster

Journal

Calendar

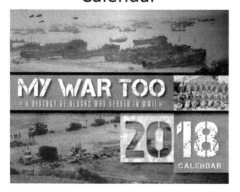

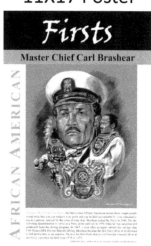

Retail $14.99
Discounted Price $5

Retail $10

Retail $10
Just Released

Journals are available at www.amazon.com.
Other products available exclusively through our website.

If you have a book to publish, email marsha@orisonpublishers.com

www.BlacksinWWii.com

Printed in the USA
CPSIA information can be obtained
at www.ICGtesting.com
LVHW080036210924
791680LV00008B/1310